THE LIVING AND THE DEAD

THE LIVING AND THE DEAD

poems by
ANN HAYES
WITH AN AFTERWORD BY JOHN HART

Carnegie-Mellon University Press
Pittsburgh & London

Acknowledgments

Acknowledgment is gratefully made to editors of the following magazines in which most of these poems first appeared:

The American Scholar, Carnegie Review, The Southern Review, Three Rivers Poetry Journal, and The Virginia Quarterly Review.

"For Sally Barnes" originally appeared as a limited edition privately printed in Pittsburgh, 1963.

"Amo Ergo Sum," "Amo Ergo Est," and the poems in Part II are reprinted from a chapbook, *The Dancer's Step*, published by Three Rivers Press. Copyright Ann Hayes, 1973.

"Grain of Stone" received a Borestone Mountain Poetry Award, and appeared in *Best Poems of 1968* published by Pacific Books, Palo Alto, California.

Library of Congress Catalog Card Number: 75-4385
ISBN 0-915604-01-9

Printed and bound in The United States of America

Contents

I
For Sally Barnes

1

The way with pain is not the way of words.
Only the searching sense is eloquent,
Asking no comfort, asking only life
To answer bone to bone and nerve to nerve
Till sighing breath draws back, and deepens, slows,
And mind lets go the consciousness of pain,
Drowsy as pleasure in recurring needs
Of food or water, sleep beyond caress,
In ways of healing flesh, enduring still
Because the flesh endures and will be met:
Absent in pain and then surprised at ease,
Worn in the course of habit, we can live
As ailing bone and nerve forget themselves,
Holding to life because they always did.

2

Knotted in other days or stretched instead,
Spun by the days that feed upon design,
O we are subtly woven, living thread,
Held for our lives to others we confine.
Only ourselves, our patterned selves at last,
Surrendering the days to meet the days,
Turning to suit the time and woven fast,
Enclose ourselves in time as time decays.
To take a breath release a breath: the last
As we had never breathed and never must,
Stirs for a moment, lives without the past,
Voiceless before it settles with the dust.
How easily it goes: a thread of air
Across a thread of days and ending there.

3

Quiet increases quiet in the snow,
As winter barren still and clinging fair,
Softly to gather, softer yet to grow,
Clasping the edge of crystal and the air.
Only the mingling cold, but water stills,
Lingers upon its course and does not fall,
Or floating slowly drifts, and settles, fills,
Separate cold that closes over all.
O but the spring of water, colorless,
Falls in a shift of liveliness and air,
Falls into rushing white, in comet dress
Gathers in rivers, spreading quiet there.
Frozen be still, and frozen still be strange,
Soft on the frozen earth to melt and change.

4

Water is rippling water: ring by ring
Shakes the reflected moon as light is shaken,
Circles of broken surface glistening,
Brilliance on brilliance from the quiet taken:
Water regaining stillness and reflection
Subsides to darker quiet and the moon
Gathering out of shadow recollection
Steadies to shadow, pours the light of noon.
Ripples are moving light and light subsiding:
Shall I be still myself, reflecting you,
Shaken with you, within myself dividing,
Finding you deep within the self I knew?
All at the heart is quiet, nothing shaken,
Still as the moon the still reflection taken.

5

Now days regain the light of various spring,
Open along the veins that lay and curled
While green on green returned across the world
Where far and briefer days of harvest cling.
Upon a mold of time the earth has spun
Substance of steady shade, a softer night,
Has grown of air and built upon the light
A flesh as cool as water, filled with sun.
So we compound the air, so tentative
We draw upon the time of summer's end,
And grow the flesh of shadows, selves to lend
The substance of our promises to live.
I know the ways of wonder and the spring:
Longer the days to take the lives they bring.

6

I reached for pain and tried to make it grow,
Thinking that I could find an end of it,
Opened myself upon it, let it go
Beyond the grasp of nerve, control of wit.
I hung upon my life and dreaded less:
I gave my flesh away and did not dream:
I knew I was not losing consciousness
And recognized my voice and heard it scream.
I shook with cold beside another grave,
Open to freezing flesh in freezing air,
And took the shelter that the living gave
In flesh alive to cold and dying there.
The dead are safe from pain and safe alone.
I shelter from the cold with flesh and bone.

7

I do not trust a word: I know the lies
Creeping upon my fingers and my nerves
And twisted into shape before my eyes
Out of a need of nothing praise deserves.
I have a lying promise to betray,
Smoother assurance than a word extends,
Sharing and shared till I must give away
Even a hope that honesty pretends.
Do not believe me then: I am not true.
My every word is murmuring with need
And would be anything to pleasure you,
Honor no more than license it would feed.
I cannot find the self that you have known
Or turn myself to that and you alone.

8

I will be gone into myself again,
Dissolve beneath the seasons of the air,
Grow soft and rich as earth whose stones contain
The terms of a performance given there.
All I can do is weighted with a breath,
Weighted with love and patiently forgone
And given up to me: the terms are death
Whose final eagerness is what is done.
We mark the dead with love, in need of love,
And time in comprehending us denies,
Takes back the legend that our hearts approve,
Its slow erasure bearing no surprise.
The grain of stone is cut and left to wear:
O name and date diminish slowly there.

9

I am soft earth and given quality
A little while for prizing, nothing more,
And yet alive as time is touching me,
O soft as breath, is brushing all before.
A little while: it wears the earth at last,
Crumbles the lines of age in soft decay,
Catches a breath indrawn and presses fast,
Closes the earth as minutes close the day.
Soft as the day's resuming, sifting on,
Shivering gold abounding in the light,
Presently dust is dancing and is gone,
Trembles to color, flickers out of sight.
O nothing more: the earth is turning gold
In glancing light the longer, growing old.

10

I am no more afraid than this, my love,
To hold my breath at night to hear a breath
Whispering soft recurrence, softly prove
Myself the source and element of death.
What need of words to give my fears excuse?
Only give back a breath that was my own,
Let pain go by in hope and hope in use,
Let be familiar, being simply known.
Let be, my love, let be: in stillness met,
Condensing terror and advancing blind,
Beneath the veil of flesh what gazes yet
When nothing breathes to calm the shuddering mind?
O, I am just the self I have to fear,
The heart alone with terror drawing near.

11

We have to be afraid: no other way,
No more to be ourselves than sweating hands
And this our shallow breath, the words we say
A tissue of protection and demands:
No more communion than infected fear,
Sharing an apprehension of the bone
To huddle in response, and drawing near
To find a comfort, sacrifice alone.
In course of living food: but so we feed,
Drawing upon each other, clinging there,
And tear ourselves away: O slake and breed,
Fulfilling emptiness, what fearful share?
In living fear of what our living means,
A shred of flesh upon the bone it cleans.

12

No patience now for pain: insensitive
Remark the angry interest of nerve
Fed on the heart's anxiety to give
And meet the terms indifference will serve.
Only be deaf and sound is powerless,
Be glazed my eyes, have nothing more to see,
Dull in the cold of such forgetfulness
Linger my senses sleeping quietly.
Open the living world and let me by,
Let me go past, I do not choose to stay,
I do not need a name, I am not I,
Close down the mask and take the mind away.
Time is the steel: our dying selves will rot
O where they joined in flesh and now are not.

13

I listened for your voice, and when it came
I listened unpersuaded of its sound,
And then took back a syllable of name
To say I was myself and you were found.
These tokens of identity! We thread
Responses to each other on demand,
With hush of words in silences of dread
Quiet the start of terror close at hand.
Let household be indefinite abyss:
We cling upon a crevice in the ice,
A glittering face of fear admitting this
In icy sweat of knowledge and device,
Letting us stretch and come to nothing there,
Mingle our lives upon the empty air.

14

Born of a little dust, a little ease
Made in the recognition of a word,
Our past of custom fills our privacies
From breath to breath in being overheard.
Both gain and loss: the intimately known
Yields to a look or gesture histories
Of reuniting love and selves alone
Wander in silence and complexities.
Where we have been is knowledge of our own
And ripened senses, time whose traces grow
The selves we have to promise and the tone
Of all we love and have in trusting so.
Responses intermingled in the nerve,
Nothing is wanted, nothing else will serve.

II
The Dancer's Step

FOR A BRASS RUBBING

Roger of Trumpyngtoun in coat of mail,
Figure in brass, intaglio and tomb,
Frowning a little waits for what's to come.
His sword remains in scabbard at his side,
His feet are crossed upon a playful dog
Curving its back, tugging the scabbard tip.
How can a death be knowing? These alive
Have sat together in some other hall,
Have kept, and keep their habit.

So he lies
As he has lain for centuries, and still
As he was lying when the pilgrims passed,
And knights among them, to the famous shrines;
As he was lying when the players passed,
Mocking from yard to innyard famous knights;
As he was lying when the roundheads came
And scraped away the others, purified,
And swept the fragments out the holy doors.
He who escaped continues as he was
To passing visitors.

Another art
Endures transference to another world.
Upon a piece of paper, silver, black,
He changes his position, looking down.
His armored fingers palm and palm in prayer,
Formal and gleaming, feet stretched out to play,
Hung on the wall he gazes as he lies,
A work of art become a work of art,
And man turned into dust those years ago,
Still in his tomb and dust those years ago.

PIETA

This figure mourns that figure hanging dead,
Each marble face an emblem, sacrifice
Born of its pity, fury seen with love.
The hammer fell upon a lifted arm,
Fell on a face, smashed at an eye, a nose.
What did he want, what did he think to kill,
What urgent holiness did he believe
Who called himself the Christ and struck at stone?

Send flowers to the altar, holy place.
New to the shock we come, we gasp and sigh,
Mourning for surface lost, for stone and light,
Waste of a passion borne and spent, of skill
That cut as surgeons cut to quicken life.
What fury held a hand as firm as stone?
What fury turned the marble into flesh?
The living and the dead, who gave us both?

The Holy Father is householder here
And is instinct to pray. O pray for us,
You who believe in prayer, to find a place
Where life embodied in the arms of love
Can mourn its dead. Madonna made of stone,
Powder of marble, dust upon the air,
We saw your face that others will not see.
Lady of griefs, what image do you keep?

FOR AN HERB BOOK, REPRINTED

Herbs of another time and place
Recall as memory a charm
Of healing, cooking, lore of grace
In old replies to human harm.

A pleasant picture book divides
Their virtue into various kinds,
The practices of each decides,
Which milk dilutes or honey binds.

Familiar plants of parsley, sage
Grown steadily across the years
In woodcuts echo on the page
The older books where each appears.

And ancient ill and ancient pain
Resist the ancient recipes
Where hope and learning meet in vain
A chronicle of miseries:

Of migraine, choler, wicked dreams
To plague the aching head of man
Who seeks a remedy that seems
As far away as it began.

Search in the garden, search the field
For betony and southernwood,
Or make the sweets of roses yield
To bring us health, to make us good.

Give cleansing leaves to pestilence,
Find seed to make the lecher chaste,
With roots turn fever into sense,
Bring fruit to wombs that yearn and waste.

Better to turn the page again,
Try recipes to season food,
For dill and bay and thyme contain
A flavor still that tasted good

In mouths that opened, laughed, and kissed
While pestilence and dream went by,
And balm that all the herbals missed
May still be growing as we die.

THE CLOISTERS: OAK CARVING

We look about the ornamented screen
In exercise of interest: we have seen
Tower and cornice, block on block of stone
That wealth has gathered for us; we have known
The impudence of choosing and the skill
Which lifted from the earth of a far hill
The pieces of a building, set them down
In purchased grace above the present town.

We wonder now who saw a chance of life
Within the solid oak, who turned a knife
And cut away unnecessary wood
For rich remains of figures understood
In prophecy and promise; scene by scene
The vision of a girl as heaven's queen
Is line and shade the gospel that he spoke
And time that passes in the grain of oak.

The panels mark the days: her birth foretold;
And here obedient child, her parents old,
Brought to the temple, yielded hand to hand;
Drawn in a fold of wood that could withstand
The years of joy and grief, could bloom and fade
In floating leaves that were a summer's shade,
She waits the messenger, the angel bent
In praise and prayer of greeting and consent.

In order then the journey and the inn,
A place of birth from which the years begin,
Herself the offertory, carven scene
Of hope and patience brought to what they mean
In dreams of women, virgin at a birth
Sung in a night of peace around the earth,
Guiltless within the joy, a living child
Laid in her arms to sleep while others smiled.

Panel by panel: but the figured cross
Will tell of noon time in a wooden gloss
Of endless days beyond the cutting knife
While men are born and die, forgotten life
Blown with the shaken leaves, the numberless
Tracing our lives to nothing we can guess
Who dream of richer dreams than virgin good
Bearing the dead upon the shining wood.

GRAIN OF STONE

1

Scatter of mica in the summer sun
Speckles with light, speckles with flaking gold,
Glitters upon the shells of other seas,
The tide of other days; and solid rock
Bears from the pressure of the shifting earth
A crystal harvest variously bright:
Transparency of water, tourmaline,
Or topaz glinting yellow, sun and shade,
Or zircon blue and green, or garnet dust,
Color and grain of semi-precious stone.

Carrara marble is the sculptor's stone.
It takes a penetration of the light
Bringing the polished surfaces alive
As skin that takes a color from the sun.
This pair of figures was a marble block,
A flawless piece that now is wounded flesh,
Its face of pity sheltering from grief
Emblem of life and death. The stone is cold
And yet the carven hand is newly dead,
The arm that holds him is alive and warm.

My eyes are warm with tears. I blink and stare,
Seeing before the alter of the dead
A woman sitting with her child again,
An open empty hand, a fallen hand
Heavy with relaxation into death.
What face of love has died while love looked on
That is not suited in the pieta?
The two are motionless, are merely stone,
As motionless as grief that sees the dead
While sorrow crawls the skin and presses home.

2

How casual the landscape of the world,
The ancient weight of hills, the spiny heights
We call proportion, measuring the sky
Where mountain masses shift to changing cloud;
And yet we mark its ways: it climbs and folds,
Intrudes, condenses, grinding stone on stone
Till crystal faces crumble, cling, compact,
Turning to thick and smooth beneath the earth,
Stone for the sculptor, stone to cut and carve,
A vein to find and quarry in the air.

Let marble be a witness to the mind,
The Parthenon a triumph that we see,
Master illusion in a perfect frame,
Control dimension by a stroke of wit.
Proportion's monument! The columned sky
Remains to mark the city on the heights,
Its long-enduring polish, curving stone
Of ancient places that the mind restores,
Though marble changes in the morning light
To take the next dimension of the past.

Stone in the quarries of Pentelicon
Was whiter once than moonlit columns now.
In rose of dawn, in gold of early sun,
In shining afternoon the days collect,
Cling like a shadow from the passing clouds,
Color of time the softest touch of air
That dresses living marble with the years
While humans crumble, and the weight of time
Is dream and ruin lives cannot repair
Though golden temples stand upon the hills.

III
A Record of Our Time

A RECORD OF OUR TIME

I: The Gorgon Head

No one believes until it happens so.
We stared at hate, we stared upon ourselves
Unterrified in wonder, standing still,
Became ourselves reflected, turned to stone,
Caught in each other's eyes our staring eyes,
Gazed at each other while our nerves grew still.
A breath and yet a breath: some living man
So used the moment of an afternoon,
Saw as he hoped the distant murdering
Reflect his heart's desire. In what face
Dread beyond action seeming like ourselves,
What steady pulse of blood that turns to stone?

We stare at public villainy and death
In that swift damage striking ruinous,
Draw for ourselves a breath of agony
That cannot know it lives a little while
Beyond the living order of the mind.
From hate to hate we take the heavy tide
And look about the business of the day
To find the criminal, forgotten blood
Roaming our hands and urging to our nerves
What fury of a man is waiting there
Restless to kill and petulant to blame,
Active for vengeance in a common hate.

A moment: it has crept into the past,
Except as horror rushes into mind,
Obliterates the passages of time
And draws our nerves together, coalesced
In guilt of what we know and what we knew
Incredible and never a surprise.
A place of history: the man is dead
And still the street is used and must be used.
We cannot stop though many men have died
And markers tell us if we glance at them,
Remembering, but passing every day
And less and less attending as we pass.

A place of history, where hate and fear
Sprang from the fixed and furious in our eyes
And hatred turns upon us gorgon sight,
Medusa grins upon us: if we turn,
Colder than snaky writhing is our fear
To see ourselves reflected in her eyes,
Our place of homage dreadful, casual,
Our beating hearts in heavy grain of stone.
A crowd of faces born to other times
Will stare at us, for we are witnesses
Whose story bears no telling: grief and hate
Our last and present license to the dead.

II: For Our Dead

1

We have a present license to the dead
In dust that rises up from day to day,
Clings to the hands, is granule to the eyes.
We did not see the coffin lowered home.
Waiting in turn above the costly ground
We search our custom for the words to say
The grave is decent and encloses him.

Alive in us who bear the mortal dust
Is sure conversion of the living world
To grassy hills of slowly sinking earth,
Our long reunion. Day returns the flesh
To losing presence, hangs upon the air
A mist of breath, a cloud of turning cold.
The curling moss had once the shape of love.

2

We feed upon ourselves, for still the pulse
Stirs and the temples beat, compresses vein,
Draws to its use the warm and fragrant air.
No one alone: and central, all alone,
The human figure dropping into dust.
A sudden interruption of event,

Part of a gesture by an empty hand,
The incomplete, the privacy of grief,
Leaches the heart to drain the life away.

Ours is the gift, for greatness in our eyes
Grows on a fatal eminence of life
Whose stature, posture, voice is known to us,
Moves in familiar ways as if unknown.
Theirs was the force and strength, their blood and bone
Beyond a citadel, in fragile shield
Housed the bright seeing and reflected it.
The gift and promise as they took their place
Became the passion of their funerals.

3

Gathered remains, our grief is yet ourselves:
For any circumstance will shrink in time,
And wonder in the nervous memory
Will shape the passing luster of a dream
As pearl is born, a creamy glint of shell
Born of the tide, the present covering
Its gleaming surfaces about the stone.
Under the patina of passing days
The violent unmeaning of the flesh.
A record of our time is washing smooth
And closing on the grain of name and date
Mingles the human with the pearly dust.

MONTGOMERY, ALABAMA: SPRING, 1961

"Love and honor and pity and pride and compassion and sacrifice" – William Faulkner

Public occasion here, and time to pause,
Call it well met: observe centennial
Together in a sacrifice of laws
Here on the streets around the terminal.
We ask for riot, will in blood discuss
What shame and scorn and pity can neglect:
Coming to see if things can change for us,
We are enduring what we should expect.
All of us bear the cost, indeed exact,
Utter a fury terrible to sustain,
Screaming that it will hurt, in fearful act
Deliver us all beneath a rage of pain.
What we destroy we are, we lose for good,
Ourselves a weapon in our common blood.

BASTILLE DAY, 1965

(For Adlai E. Stevenson)

No voice is true to sing him safely home
Or break a silence with the sound of grief.
The elegy, although we speak his words,
Is foreign to his sense: we cannot mourn
With leaves of bay and myrtle, for his face
Looks out with laughter from the accolade,
Enduring open-eyed the tribute given
Only for sake and dignity of love.

Chances accepted in convention hall
Are yet the shades and partisans of hope
That did not give him office, let him serve.
He spoke to us, the non-political
Born to the fortune of our own disdain,
And measured a dimension of the state
To praise integrity, the private face
That dares to be the face the public sees.

Our tyrannies dissolve into each other.
With lips of frozen gold and frozen eyes
Under the pluck and grasp of Midas hand
We let a decade die. No healing search
Of wit to answer our imagining:
We hid ourselves in comfort, growing rich,
Hating our secret knowledge that the world
Whispered its vision of the asses' ears.

We celebrate the day the prison fell,
An ancient dream of freedom, and we dream
Of human strength to bear its frailty
And hold the terror back, though history
Is knowledge that we cannot turn the scales
Or learn to balance justice with our love:
And we live on to bear the weight of hope,
Though proven mortal in a London street.

The day is ending, pales the farthest sky.
He lived the morning, visited with friends,
And kept engagements. We can see his face
Who lived for almost all the summer day,
And hear his voice, who in the morning said
His final public words, familiar tones
Intelligence concerned, conjecturing
While death and silence moved within his veins.

THE ELEMENT OF FIRE

1

A century in balance, here or there
To fall as force provides: we did our work,
We shook their bones to ashes, cloud of flame,
And made the terms of peace. Our cities stand
Untouched by bombers though the bombers flew,
And still untouched although the cities burn.

Fire in London, marshals by the Thames
Are walls and men of any city streets,
Frankfort and Coventry and Rotterdam,
But smoke is thickest over German ground
And islands of the far Pacific sea.
There on the empty beaches moves the shade.

A silt of bone and ashes turns to root
In mysteries of guilt where churches feed
And stores and schools and houses grow again.
The cities prosper: humming summer bees
Draw from the crowded hearts they visit there
No poisoned honey but their daily lives.

2

Shall we have words for any other years?
Ours is a century of famous names
But not of persons: places where they were
Are memories of names we do not say
When ordinary towns they might have been
Have turned to Auschwitz, Belsen, Buchenwald.

Take Hiroshima out of memory,
And Nagasaki; Stalingrad; Kiev;
Warsaw; Coblenz; Tokyo: all who burned.
Seal up Tarawa of the leafless palms,
Close fast the mouths of Iwo Jima's caves
Where men did not surrender, flamed and died.

Let centuries reduce to elements
And ours is fire, ours the stripping flame.
Combustion and explosion, these our tools,
Our force of ease and power, toy of speed,
Our bravery of skill in heavy smoke
Haunting the empty sky we cannot burn.

3

Fire enclosed the martyrs. Frightened men
Knew wood beneath their feet and watched a torch:
And other hands have carved in other wood
As if they had not changed, as if in fact
They line the doors of centuries, their flame
A place of memory, a certain life.

What fire burned upon an ancient hearth
And signaled victory from hill to hill?
We have no glory: at Thermopylae
Did they believe their saying? Men who died
Created centuries that we have lived
But ours the fortune of their epitaphs.

For those who kneel in flames, for those who dare,
What private terror in the market place
Will light the space around them till they die?
The villages that know the sound of death
Wait for an answer, wait in smoky day
Their random singling out, their scattered pyres.

And ashes of the martyrs blow away,
O for them only! Dust that circles still
Drifting the wind from any place of death,
Blown upon any street we have to take
Is memory anonymous and vain,
The air we know polluted as we breathe.

HANDY-DANDY

"Look with thine ears; see how yond justice rails
upon yond simple thief. Hark, in thine ear: change
places, and, handy-dandy, which is the justice,
which is the thief?"

King Lear, IV, vi.

1

For A Disciplinary Committee

We sit perplexed among our decencies.
Hoping to make all even, we would mend,
Smoothly would weave to make the patches serve.
Facing these eyes, facing these nervous mouths,
We would repeat the patterns we have tried.
We ask our questions, fearful of their fears,
Anxious, awaking terror. No man learns
What he does not already know, they say.

The ancient tree grows tall, the roots reach down,
Bright fruit hangs ready: in this ornament
We figure generations of dismay.
Startled to hear a voice, each child looks up,
Guilty by accusation. Lonely men
Cannot recall when loneliness began
Or make the serpent speak. What old regrets
Wait beyond sleep at night to call a name?

Our slight misdeeds, these small injustices,
This nameless commonsense that smooths the way,
These bore no tag until the hand came down,
Were priced at nothing till the sheriff called.
I was asleep before the dream began,
The solid earth fell back, the darkness came.
If I could speak, my love would answer me.
Out of my mouth there bursts the nightmare scream.

To this we answer: for a while be good,
Do not come back. Although it's in the file,
No record follows when you graduate.
You'll see us here and there but we forget.
Probation. We will send the notice home.
They pay your bills, they'd think us much to blame
If there's a second action and you fail.
This is our judgment but you may appeal.

2

Londonderry Sunday

We have seen it all before.
Crowd is coming down the street.
Nervous soldiers wait. They meet.
Sticks and stones and something more.

Sudden fire, sudden death,
Ending that we did not mean.
Air is gas and dirt's unclean.
Dive for shelter. Gasp for breath.

Lift the dying, stagger, die.
Blood is in the puddles still.
Hate and anger suck their fill.
Rage comes up to drink them dry.

"On their graves I'll shed no tear.
We shall mark revenges down . . ."
Set the torch about the town.
Soldiers killed. Let soldiers fear.

Sunday's coming round again.
Bloody Sunday: maybe twice
We'll assist at sacrifice.
What can stop us? Who'll refrain?

Law was made to save from grief.
You may tremble, we have guns,
Shoot for blood: and so it runs,
Which the justice, which the thief?

MUCH ADO ABOUT NOTHING, THANKSGIVING, 1972

They have a few amusements, presidents,
Drop into restaurants they used to like
After the secret service clears the way;
Simpler, I guess, to stay at home with friends,
Open the bourbon there and talk and laugh;
And yet sometimes a public man can wish
To have the pleasant time the public has.
The Nixons took a moment of success
After election, easy mandate in,
After Thanksgiving with the country safe.
Public and private, New York theater,
They made a party: men in business suits,
His wife beside him, Bebe, both the girls,
All shining, smiling, waving, shirted, furred;
And other men who kept their backs to him
Sat nearby on the aisles and looked at us.
The play was a success but nothing nude
And nothing controversial: current hit,
Shakespeare revived and made American.

The plot of *Much Ado*? Old foolishness,
Old tales again: young men returned from war
Into a merry war, to laughing trials
Of wit upon each other, brothers' quarrels,
A hidden search for love: though much ado,

Nothing it is, a smiling social world
Where everyone observes and masquerades
And some who speak the truth have wounding tongues.
Remember noting? Semblances and lies
Are false belief and action spied upon,
Accomplished plots deliberately played.
You do remember innocence ashamed,
Shallow though it may be, yet lost, disgraced,
Begrimed by a pretense. But there's the Watch
Who catch the villains though they cannot tell
Flat burglary from slander, muddle all
Until frustration tells the truth of crime:
Eavesdropping, lies, deception and pretense,
A comedy before our president.

I watched him watch. I was across the aisle
A row away, with murder in my heart
Though he was safe with me, needed no men
To stand between his beating heart and mine.
I would not touch him. But I shook with hate
And horror at my hatred, not so felt
Until I stood so near: the bitter years,
How they had prospered him! I told the names
For slandered lives behind him. Did they hate?
Surely they tasted acid I could taste.
How well he played on fear, how well he knew
What we would shudder from, what we'd protect.

Meanwhile the play was playing: Benedick
Swore that he'd been defamed by Lady Tongue,
The audience saw through and laughed him down.
Did Warren hate him? In that old campaign
When votes were traded and the big chance came,
What was a promise? Warred understood,
That I believe, and left him to contempt.

We who can see the cast and feel the spell
Continuously unwinding, shall we know
The justice from the thief? I watched and he,
Gazed at the constables who brought the law,
Gazed at a show of penitence and grief.
Now can we tell deception, now be sure
Which friend to trust, which bride to bring to bed?
There was applause and laughter, there was love
Successfully recovered, partners found
And all put right within a little world
Where old, old instances remain to mock
But wit can still be true. We turned to him,
Turned from the bowing stage to see his bow,
And some applauded loud but others hissed,
Others like me, even in that success,
We hissed and cried at him. He took our cries,
He smiled and waved, he made the outrage last.
World of good neighbours lost, I heard my voice,
Liar, it cried, liar, you lie, you lie.

IV
The Amo Poems

AMO ERGO SUM

1

This calm is grown of trust: the city ways
Are empty of all others, just alight,
And nothing follows on the steps of sound.
But wakeful to your sense, alive in you
And leisurely in breath and even pulse
The unaccustomed pace that is our own.

Walking through shadows of forgotten size,
We move together down an avenue,
The privacy of others giving place.
Each motion is the evidence of trust
And confidence of order: all the world
Shudders in balance on the dancer's step,
Accepts itself upon a moment's grace,
Remembers what it is to breathe again.

2

Heart of the fruit has flowered, was a day
When petals opened wide beneath the sun
And fragrance hung upon a milder air
Spun with the beating wings, transparency
A weight of sweetness on the silken bloom.
In shape of brilliant fruit, returning flesh

Changes the various colors of the light
To smoothly stretching skin, to seed and stem,
Distilling summer to formality,
Itself the shadow and the gift of time.

A breath that comes and goes: what edge of pain
Moves in the stirring wind as petals drift,
Flake from the shivering stem the curling rose?
Current of seasons, irresistible,
Moves in the placid air of summer night:
Form upon form, self upon self is lost
Without regret or haste, without surprise,
Borne upon joy a moment balancing,
Still in the moment waiting other selves
As shadowed being folds upon itself,
Bearing in living flesh the living mind.
Nothing is equal: being in its time
Most absolute of possibilities,
Reflecting light a moment, passes by
Even as drops of rain to spring and fall
In pattern on the ground of promises.

I thought of quiet: in the falling rain
The separate present drops identical.
I thought of quiet: murmurings of mind
Only myself and inadvertent pain,
And worst of guilt the usual mischance.

Self upon self the grave and ghost remain:
Now in the shaking quiet of the night
Alone myself unequal to myself
I watch the shadows measuring the light.

3

I have a dream of grief, a dream of love:
Awakening at morning from the past,
No more than dream a sleeping night away,
No more than recognition that I am,
I search across my senses: memory,
Identity I put aside with sleep,
Awaits repeated sound, whose echo then
Is reassurance of a history,
Today secure upon a yesterday,
A shadow of the time unquieted.

I have a dream of grief, a dream of love:
Even as breath upon the lips of sleep
Draws in and out upon its hidden ways,
Catches with pain and wakens into tears,
I have a dream of substance turning real,
Amassed beyond the mind's capacity,
Born into weight and size, and taking shape,
Dream without place, without alternative,
At rest upon the heart of sacrifice,
The living flesh within the reach of time.

4

The offices of love are left to me
Because I will observe them as I am.
So I observe that self and self are true
When hope of loving and the act of love
Mingle with breath a moment to respond.
So I observe I am: and must draw near
Beyond the shadows of alternative;
And I observe for love and charity
The gentleness of health, the lively thought,
The brave creation I would still confess
For love and charity: death comes to this,
For knowledge is as separate from will
As I am from myself in saying so,
But I will not deny the thing I know.

I am my body: be it taken then
For I am given as I give my word.
I am my blood: a channeling of time
However slight or fine its dwelling place
Instinct with life or death. I know it lives:
Answers more swiftly than the busy nerve
By willing enterprise can call it back.
I know it lives: obliterating sense
Comes with the mercy of the passionate
To take away the knowledge of itself
Crowding the instant from the sense of time.
What shall I do? My body and my blood
Created life exactly images
The unimagined infinite alone.

5

The day of dying, shadowing the ground,
Is absolute forever in the mind,
Measuring light against oblivion
In patient circles turning into time:
A moment without shadow, stroke of noon,
Steadily grows the length of any day.

And ordinary progress of the sun
Is yet a day that waits incredible
And does not reoccur and only is.
In this reunion we take up our lives
To meet ourselves and find upon our lips
Our living promises to bless and praise.

In this reunion, in the crossing point
Of time that simply was and always is,
Beyond the ceremony of the fact,
Be curious and sad: awake again,
Puzzle a little and forget and grieve
The minutes turning hours into years.

In this reunion, in the crossing point
Of hand on hand supported, lifted, given,
My dear, in flesh upon the marks of time,
Upon the interlacing crevices
Of sweating skin and nerve, accept today
Our human love and its mortality.

AMO ERGO EST

1

Dark in the riddle lies the seed of fear,
Alive within the patient enterprise
Of many centuries to speak of it,
To find enclosing flesh of certainty:
Borne on the wind of breath, the centuries
Cut into stone a shape to wear away.

Dark in the riddle: painful every day
The old give up their places wretchedly
And children see the sacrifice to come
With eyes that do not see, expect reprieve.
In place of certainty the patient bones
Come walking to the marble of the grave
As if the minute held necessity
To be in time and patient then to die.

2

Offer the shape of beauty to the air,
Born of a river, of a widening pool
Under a shining rock where water spills
Smooth as the light and irresistible
Pulled by the turning earth, itself the tide
Under the turning faces of the moon,

Unmeasuring: and measurable time
Smoothing away, smoothing the rock away
Murmurs along the seas unnoticing
Till all the shining surfaces are bare.

Offer the turning faces of the moon
Caught in the deepest stillness of the pool
Moved by the flickering life that swims and feeds,
Lives on the light and shade of passing time.
The faces do not see: the moon reflects
Seeming to touch the water and the stone.
Only the night remains: the quiet dark
To pass in shadows as the hours pass,
Letting a pale inquiry of the moon
Shiver upon the water wakening
A penetration and a space of stars,
To fade before the dawn, dissolve in air
Upon the moving river motionless.

Only the night, the sleeping face of love,
Holds yet within its quiet surfaces
Seeming to trust, seeming to offer then
Untouchable its beauty open-eyed.
Beneath the pleasures of the yearning hand
In gentle touch awakening to be,
The soft persuasions of a murmuring
Mount and fulfill in passionate reply.

Illusion then the knowledge of our love,
Reflected as the moon, unmeasuring:
Out of our need each other's answering,
Our faces that we turn and turn away.

3

Look for the dead to walk again alive.
Wait and be glad to see the face of love,
Familiar eyes of knowledge, mouth to kiss.
Listen to hear the well-remembered step.
O they will move, will stir the quiet grass
Created of their shelter and repose,
Their incomplete advancing still in flesh,
Searching in earnest with a seeming eye,
Terrible in the beauty of the world
To see their places filled by living men.

Look for the dead to walk again alive.
With custom and propriety of rite
Offer to habit the intolerable;
Manage from breath to breath to find and say
The ordinary and the proper words,
Murmur of common anguish and reply
In requiem the living and the dead.
We have no more: the open hand of time,
And all our works, the stone to bear our names,
Bear witness to the passing of the days.

4

We greet and mark with news of sacrifice
The coming of the stranger and the child
With ceremony then to give ourselves
Before the faces watching shadowy
Against a fear ourselves will offer him.
In random passages of memory,
Inhabiting a breath, discovery
Enclosing and forlorn, what hope can live
To wear the dress and privilege of time?
Ever the breath of promise comes and goes
And speechless love must hold its breath to see
If life comes sighing back or drifts away,
And yet endure the riddled answering
Forsaken then of all remembering.

What ceremony else for innocence?
The hands of death hold fast, and younger hands
Wring from each other every gift of need.
O cry upon our lives their sacrifice,
Grow blind to see the courage made of love
Take up and bear the lives we give away.
No more than awkward flesh in quiet space
Casual, final, at the heart of time,
Ourselves to give the promises of love,
Ourselves in need of brief identity
To be the gift, to be the offering:
Ourselves the price and need of sacrifice
Unknowing who we are become ourselves
Reflected as the image of our love.

5

In mark of tides that draw upon the shore,
Creating substance in a ritual
Of various repetition, patiently,
We watch the days come on, the gradual days,
Give and take back again our promises,
In hush and whisper of assenting mind.

So changes of the light seem orderly
As we observe with beauty in our eyes
A grace of being whose repeated forms
Grow upon nervous mind their own repose,
Incredible as love or beauty then
Within the world of our imagining.

Given the moment of creating love,
Gazing astonished in the sunny day,
Astonished in the shadow of the stars,
A dream of beauty in the forming wave
A substance then to draw upon our love
And touch the heart by what it cannot see:

Given the moment of creating love,
All else proceeds: the unimagined pace
Of all dimension suddenly to be,
To meet ourselves in substance of our hope,
Ourselves imagined and our images
A dark and fair division into time.

V
Design in the Amo Poems

an essay by John Hart

Design in the Amo Poems

I

1

Amo Ergo Sum and *Amo Ergo Est* are companion poems about love as sign of existence and force in the world. *Amo Ergo Sum* in some respects is easier and more manageable, for it is the identification of two observable phenomena, one the presence of a moment (or a finite period of time) in which love is felt and seen and known by the narrator to be truth and reality and life; the other, the presence of change and alteration and death in all things, including the narrator. These phenomena are universally felt by any sensitive person and hence are familiar and easily communicable to the reader.

The first section of *Amo Ergo Sum* describes a walk through city streets of two lovers at an hour, presumably deep in the night, when the streets are quiet and empty of people, and the only life is the life the lovers provide, moving in harmony and order; the lovers also compel the whole world to stop its restless bustle, to become part of that harmony and graceful movement. This is its natural condition of grace, called back to that state from its frantic whirling by the presence of love experienced by the lovers. Love, then, performs the function not only of providing an ecstasy of harmony and grace for each of the two lovers but of bringing the whole world also into that sphere and under the control of love.

That is the way, at any rate, it seems to the narrator. Yet looked at from another point of view, the relationship between lovers and world may be just the opposite. The second section of the poem considers this possibility. It observes the beauty of nature, the "Heart of the fruit," "the curling rose" with fragrance and sweetness come into being, brought into shape and form by summer, just as, though the reference is unstated or oblique, the love described in the first section has come into being. But each moment of time brings changes in the form so that a new and different identity is brought to the beautiful natural object, and "self upon self is lost Without regret or haste, without surprise, Borne upon joy a moment balancing." When one stands outside the beautiful object watching it grow and blossom and die, one sees it as a creature of time, a marker of the seasons, a shadow by which time is measured, but clearly no match for the world, only the beautiful victim. And the terrifying question that inevitably suggests itself is whether the certainty and the supremacy of the moment of love described in the first section is not exactly like that: a marker of the seasons, a shadow by which time is measured. The narrator, alone in the quiet of the night, has this vision borne in strongly to the mind. And *quiet,* which characterized the whole world in the first section and was a symbol of the triumph of love, is now changed to a "shaking quiet" in which only the awareness of succeeding selves, moment by moment, remains; and the narrator is out of balance, a painful participant and partner with the rest of the shadows which are "measuring the light," the passage of time.

Section 3 of *Amo Ergo Sum* continues in two ways from Section 2. One is that the narrator is still alone, the other is that the time is the awakening from the sleep so long in coming in Section 2. The first stanza of Section 3 gives detailed recounting of the phenomena attached to waking up: the recovery of one's identity (for which familiar sounds and surroundings are a necessity) and the resumption of conscious memory so that today is "secure upon a yesterday". Both time and place are needed to establish identity; they are conditions which at once confirm the observation made in the second section that one is a victim, a slave of time, but also make it possible for anyone to have identity at all.

But then there is the dream, the intervening time between consciousness at night and awakening in the morning. Even as the breath in sleep goes quietly onward measuring the passage of time, there is "a dream of substance turning real, Amassed beyond the mind's capacity," a dream not describable as awakening is by place or memory but only there, "At rest upon the heart of sacrifice." Thus, in the midst of the wearing away of the narrator by time, the sacrifice of all things to time, there at the heart, at rest, is the "dream of grief," synonomous with the "dream of love," which the ecstatic moment of love epitomized in the first section of the poem.

The last line of the section takes on an ambiguity which reflects the contrary observations of the whole poem so far. "The living flesh within the reach of time" is the life in nature at the command, at the control of time; it repeats the phrase of the second section which is describing how "self upon self is lost" as time goes on. At the same time, in the context of Section 3, it is "the living flesh" of the dream, which takes on reality within the reach of but not the control of time, for its laws are different from time or place, a reality with its own existence and its own laws.

The narrator, in the fourth section of *Amo Ergo Sum,* accepts the contradictory phenomena of the first three sections but will not be paralysed or neutralized by them. In fact, the narrator affirms the dream, and in observing the offices of love, affirms the truth of the self by mingling the hope of loving and the act of love with the breath that measures time. And the narrator observes the reality of self, observes that that reality goes "Beyond the shadows of alternative," just as the dream in the third section was without alternative. The narrator gives all the qualities of life to love, even though death comes to life in time, because "I will not deny the thing I know."

And so the narrator offers both body and blood to love. Body is given to the lover; blood is remarked on as living, not only living but beyond the power of the "busy nerve" to control it, not only living but so powerful it can master, even overwhelm the mind, and in fact, the whole organism, "Crowding the instant from the sense of time." That is to say, blood is like the ecstatic moment of love in the first section, like the dream of love in the third section, in that its instant of reality eludes the slavery of time. And in this way the narrator's body and blood mirror the phenomena of the ecstatic moment of love and the dream of love which assert the triumph over time that can not be taken in by the conscious mind, "The unimagined infinite alone."

Section 5 draws the poem to a close, generalizing the contradictory phenomena experienced and described in the earlier sections, and bringing the relationship between the lovers to a quiet acceptance. But it also introduces the dimension of death, which had been present though muted in the earlier sections. The day of dying is as much a reality as the moment of love, and it is bound up with the "patient circles turning into time." The moment of love, like the shadowless moment of the day, is measured and changed by the growing shadows of the day which eventually will become the oblivion of night. And yet each day, despite its slavery to time, is like the ecstatic moment of love, unique, irreplaceable, a day that "only is." In this unique day, there is a reunion of the lovers that is unique: "To meet ourselves and find upon our lips Our living promises to bless and praise." But this is not merely a reunion of the lovers; it is also a union of the ecstatic moment of love with the day of dying, and a union of both of them with the unique day, a union that takes place in the crossing point of time that simply was (the moment of love on the city streets in the first section, for instance) and always is (the moment of love beyond time, "Beyond the ceremony of the fact"). Given the recognition of the reunion, not of time, but of hand on hand, the narrator urges the lover to "accept today Our human love and its mortality." Despite the inexorableness of time, *Amo Ergo Sum*, I love, therefore I am.

2

This paraphrase leaves unsaid many things. The development of images through the poem is worthy of specific analysis: the breath, the dancer's balance, the shadows, the measuring of the light, are only instances of images which take on dimension and complication as the poem goes on. And the structure of the poem suggests far more complicated organization than the paraphrase has indicated. But there is one dimension contributed by both imagery and structure that is only gradually apparent as the poem develops. This dimension is first called to our attention in a striking way in the third section of the first poem with the lines at the end:

Dream without place, without alternative,
At rest upon the heart of sacrifice,
The living flesh within the reach of time.

"The heart of sacrifice" is religious in reference, and it broadens the sense of dream from a purely personal experience to an experience including all the ritual of religious sacrifice. This framework is enlarged still further by the references to body and blood which are the central gifts to the loved one, formalized in the term "The offices of love" with which the fourth section of the first poem opens, and generalized into an image of the whole world in the last lines of Section 4:

My body and my blood
Created life exactly images
The unimagined infinite alone.

And the religious framework is reinforced once more in the last section of the poem in references to "this reunion," in which "we . . . find upon our lips Our living promises to bless and praise," that is, at least one attitude of prayer; reinforced again "In this reunion, in the crossing point" (with its glancing reference to the cross) "Of time that simply was and always is": that is, time that marked an event in history such as the death of Christ in conjunction with the continuing renewal of that event in religious rites; reinforced again, in this reunion, in the crossing point "Of hand on hand supported, lifted, given" – gestures suggestive of traditional religious services. The reunion of the lovers becomes in effect a joining of time and space and prayer in a context of religious images adding their dimension to the nature of the love described. One way to describe the love felt by the narrator is to say that it is felt as religious experience; this is suggested by the religious images which grow in strength through the poem. Another way to describe it is to suggest that love described and felt by participants in religious experience is the same kind of love felt by the narrator in this poem – I love, therefore I am.

II

Amo Ergo Est has as its starting place the moment of death and the fear surrounding it. It is a more explicit and fuller statement of the lines in the last section of *Amo Ergo Sum*:

> The day of dying, shadowing the ground,
> Is absolute forever in the mind.

Death is the riddle, and fear attaches itself naturally to the riddle, remaining alive in spite of all of man's efforts to explain death and to find a kind of certainty that would soothe or diminish or eliminate "the seed of fear." The only certainty we can see is the steady wearing away of stones intended to memorialize the dead. But that is the long view, the view of one who has stood in ancient graveyards and noticed the wind blow over the gravestones. Looked at from the present moment, one sees the old give up places they had held, wretchedly, and sees children who have before their eyes the sight of the old dying day by day without really ever taking in the phenomenon and without seeing themselves as part of the process. In the sense that death is a giving up of life by the living, it is seen as a sacrifice to which every person must come. We bury our dead; we do not know how else to memorialize our grief but by a ritual; but we are, even in the process of burying our loved ones, simply "patient bones" necessarily held in time; but when the minute of our lives is up ("minute" also carrying an overtone, touched lightly on, of record of our lives), we are patient then to die ourselves. "Patient" carries with it, both in the last line and in the earlier line, heavy emphasis on bearing or enduring suffering or pain.

The riddle then is the riddle of death, of its meaning, of its relationship to lives that have been lived and their meaning, of the steady procession of lives and generations who go to the grave to bury their loved ones, scarcely realizing that they are being held in time for a moment but are actually visiting their future homes.

The second section presents a contrast to the unfailing moment of death which constitutes the riddle of Section 1. The narrator describes a night scene in nature, a scene of beauty in which the moon, reflected in water and rock, presents a generally lifeless "unmeasuring," "unnoticing" world with only a "flickering life" and lifeless faces of the moon as participants in the scene. The scene is to be measured, is to be noticed, is to be recognized as "flickering life" but not from within it. The opening word "offer" (repeated), and the use of the words "shape," "measurable," "The faces do not see," and "reflects" give emphasis to the emptiness of the scene and the need for an outside observer to read it, to take in the beauty of the scene, to interpret it in relation to time. The word "offer" is a most striking one in this instance; it suggests the imperative but as imploring or calling attention to rather than commanding; but it is so lightly imperative that it might also be read as declarative, a simple statement with an implied "we" as subject, as if the narrator were saying that we create "the shape of beauty," we create "the turning faces of the moon." The effect of the ambiguity is that the impulse to give meaning to the scene is strong, but the recognition of illusion is strongly present too: "Only the night remains." For the narrator the best guide to meaning is not beauty nor the majesty of the outside world but time, the steady changing from hour to hour of shades of light which are measurable and real and give, if anything does, meaning to the moon and the water and the relationships of objects in space.

And this description of the external world becomes a metaphor for the relationship between the lovers. The night gives to lovers an interpretation, a meaning to their love, but the love is only "Seeming to trust, seeming to offer then Untouchable its beauty open-eyed." The passion is there, and the passionate response; but it is illusion, it is unmeasuring, it is "Reflected as the moon." And the lovers, like the faces of the moon that do not see, have faces "that we turn and turn away."

This second section reinforces the first section of this poem and contrasts with the opening sections of the first poem. The riddle of death contains within it a wondering whether life has any meaning, whether it is simply a construction, just as the beauty of the night world may be illusion, just as "the knowledge of our love" may be an illusion, so that there is nothing meaningful in any circumstance, except the impulse to "offer" a meaning coming out of each of us. The first section of *Amo Ergo Sum* affirmed the reality of the love and the trust that is bred by it as well as the power of that love to dominate the world; here it simply cites the night as holding its beauty "Seeming to trust" and pronounces the "knowledge of our love" an "illusion." And in the second section of the first poem, we have a description of life, changing from form to form, but still in all those forms, life, "Borne upon joy a moment balancing," standing in complete contrast with the external night world which is unmeaning. And in the last half of the second section of the first poem, the narrator is unable to reclaim the moment of love because of isolation, of separation, of aloneness; in this section, however, the lovers are together but the "knowledge of our love" is not.

The third section of *Amo Ergo Est* goes back to the subject of death, this time to give emphasis to our yearning to see and be with people we have loved but who have died. The idea touches on an emotion familiar enough to us, but it confronts the reader with the horrifying vision of what it would be like if it were actually to occur. The anticipation is joyous and arises out of the impulse to love, the yearning to be with the loved one. The brief exclamation "O" highlights the anticipation ("Borne upon joy a moment balancing") which swiftly gives way to the nightmare of what the reality would be: "Their incomplete advancing," "Searching in earnest with a seeming eye."

The second stanza of the third section deals with the resolution man finds for this double phenomenon of yearning and horror. He clothes the intolerable thought of an actual return of the loved ones from the dead with "custom and propriety of rite," with "The ordinary and the proper words," with requiem for "the living and the dead." Man can do no more.

Yet the same verbal mood exists in this section as in the second section. "look for," (twice), "wait," "be glad," "listen," "offer," "manage": imperatives, pleadings, group wishes, plural implied declaratives. The yearning is there so strongly that it creates the rituals, the customs that go with treatment of the dead, just as the yearning went into the creation of meaning and beauty in external nature. Section 3 then is a reinforcement of the "riddle" of the first section, just as the "dream of love" in the third section of the first poem was a reinforcement of the moment of love in the first section of the first poem.

And Section 4 holds a place comparable to that of Section 4 in the first poem. For here again in the face of the devastating emptinesses of the first three sections, countered only by the yearning insistence that the emptinesses must have meaning, comes action, comes whatever tentative cry there is that man intends to go on, to impose order and form, to give shape and meaning, however uncertain and unsure of himself he may be. The opening of the passage describes a kind of initiation rite in which "the stranger and the child" are brought within the group. The scene suggests a church and baptism but it might be any ceremony of admission. The rite is accompanied by "news of sacrifice" which makes sense out of the initiation into the group. Fear exists in us ("Dark in the riddle lies the seed of fear") which we hide, try not to communicate, using the ceremony as a distraction. Yet it is impossible to disguise this fear, for we have it in memory and are constantly discovering it, and we thus automatically know the answer to the question: "what hope can live To wear the dress and privilege of time?" Love must always be awaiting the death of the loved one, listening for the nighttime breathing of a loved child or a lover, yet knowing that such reassurance is not sufficient to give any other than the inevitable denial of hope, and that sleep with its steady breathing is yet a reminder of the riddle of death, reinforcing through sleep "Forsaken then of all remembering" the inevitability and in fact the imminence of death.

What we propose as action, then, in the face of death is ceremony. But we become so involved in ceremony and so fearful of death that to others we become only the formal aspect of ourselves; and we do this out of our need for holding on to each other, out of our recognition that each life is a sacrifice, out of trying to see (and of failing to see too) the courage in people who help others for love. Out of the bits of flesh we are, we become promises of love and seekers for identity and we try to be the gift, the offering to others. Out of those extensions of ourselves, which reflect both the price of sacrifice and the need of sacrifice, the ceremonies result in our not any longer being ourselves but only a reflection, an image of our love. Thus, unlike the generous gift-sharing of the narrator's body and blood in Section 4 of the first poem, this section expresses only fear which we try to cover or counter

by the introduction of ritual and ceremony to express our love and reassure each other.
Section 5 sums up the ideas expressed in the first four sections and then moves to its own conclusion from them. The tides are a way of marking the passage of time and they make their mark, "Creating substance in a ritual Of various repetition," creating, that is, literally a substance of sea materials which is deposited on the shore in a steady repeated process which by its repetition becomes a rite of nature; in addition, the process is a metaphor for the process we observe in ourselves as the days go by, wherein we are given the gifts of our promises but have them taken away again just as surely. Just as the tides mark surely the passage of time, so changes in the world afford certain beauty for us, again a kind of ritual, which provides for a naturally volatile mind an aura of sense, needing only our reaching out for it and our appreciation of it to create its own reality in our minds.

The moment of creating love, then, has power through order and ritual to create other things, "A dream of beauty in the forming wave," "A substance then to draw upon our love" or as in the last stanza, "The unimagined pace Of all dimension suddenly to be"; and in fact, from the moment of creating love comes "Ourselves imagined and our images" and any meaningful way of understanding the formulation (either dark or fair) of time. In short, I love, therefore the loved one, the external world, events in the past – everything – exists.

2

Amo Ergo Est is more elliptical, more condensed, less grammatically sortable than *Amo Ergo Sum.* Many images which carry extensions of meaning beyond the more or less straightforward thread I have followed are there in the poem. But the religious overtones are stressed, especially in reference to the rituals that are called upon as the means we use to overcome our fears of death and its unknown consequences. The first section of the poem describes the ritual of religious burial, with the living performing such rites as they can think of to memorialize the dead, though any effort is doomed to extinction, though every gesture is merely a preliminary visitation of the living to their own graves.

In the third section the narrator introduces a high and most exhilarating religious idea – that of resurrection. But the idea takes on its reality because we clothe it in "custom and propriety of rite," disguise the other intolerable reality of death and dissolution; and so we have "The ordinary and the proper words," adjectives descriptive of parts of the Mass, and we have the words of requiem spoken for both "the living and the dead." Again in the fourth section, the ceremony of baptism (or other religious initiation rite) is the same kind of formal ritual born of fear of death. Hope alone can not live "To wear the dress and privilege of time"; we need more formality and ritual than that, for there is not enough in us of reality or confidence to provide any assurance for those coming after us whom we love. And in the last section, we are said to create "substance in a ritual Of various repetition," and observe "A grace of being whose repeated forms Grow upon nervous mind their own repose." The form of ritual and liturgy becomes a reality out of our own fears and concerns and is communicated by repetition of years and ages. Out of a need to protect our loved ones from our fears, we create a reality of form, a "substance in a ritual," which is a belief in the resurrected God, so that in this religious sense, the title is "I love, therefore He is."

The two poems *Amo Ergo Sum* and *Amo Ergo Est* are both religious poems, each with different emphasis, each reflecting a different but quite legitimate religious point of view. The former starts from the gift of oneself that comes with loving, the offering of one's self, body and blood, to the loved one and to all others, this whole impulse growing out of feeling for and reaching out for one's fellow man. The latter starts from the limitations and shortness of life and our fears of death, and it develops the need to overcome these awarenesses by loving others; by clothing the awfulness of death in ceremony, by dedicating new-born life to living and social ceremony; and then it concludes with the realization that creating love gives us a chance to give everything meaning. In a way, the two poems describe the difference between the liturgy of the Mass which gives emphasis to the shared communion of the participants (*Amo Ergo Sum*), and the liturgy of the Mass which gives emphasis to the passion and death and mystery of Christ's life and death (*Amo Ergo Est*).

CARNEGIE-MELLON POETRY

The Living and the Dead, Ann Hayes (1975)

In the Face of Descent, T. Alan Broughton (1975)